T0006858

XANAX COWBOY

XANAX COWBOY

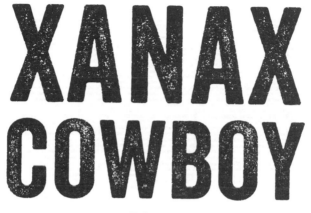

POEMS

HANNAH GREEN

ANANSI

Copyright © 2023 Hannah Green

Published in Canada in 2023 and the USA in 2023 by House of Anansi Press Inc.
houseofanansi.com

All rights reserved. No part of this publication may be reproduced or transmitted in any form or by any means, electronic or mechanical, including photocopying, recording, or any information storage and retrieval system, without permission in writing from the publisher.

House of Anansi Press is a Global Certified Accessible™ (GCA by Benetech) publisher. The ebook version of this book meets stringent accessibility standards and is available to students and readers with print disabilities.

27 26 25 24 23   1 2 3 4 5

Library and Archives Canada Cataloguing in Publication

Title: Xanax cowboy / Hannah Green.
Names: Green, Hannah (Author of Xanax cowboy), author.
Description: Includes bibliographical references.
Identifiers: Canadiana (print) 20220477108 | Canadiana (ebook) 20220477132 |
ISBN 9781487011154 (softcover) | ISBN 9781487011161 (EPUB)
Classification: LCC PS8613.R44 X36 2023 | DDC C811/.6—dc23

Cover and book design: Alysia Shewchuk

House of Anansi Press is grateful for the privilege to work on and create from the Traditional Territory of many Nations, including the Anishinabeg, the Wendat, and the Haudenosaunee, as well as the Treaty Lands of the Mississaugas of the Credit.

 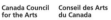

With the participation of the Government of Canada
Avec la participation du gouvernement du Canada | Canadä

We acknowledge for their financial support of our publishing program the Canada Council for the Arts, the Ontario Arts Council, and the Government of Canada.

Printed and bound in Canada

For my parents & grandparents—
the living, late & all of you great

Tell me the story of lonely and I'll show you the pain of getting clean.

—Amigo the Devil

U

Xanax Cowboy is a joke I tell myself. I am nude
in leather boots, a bolo tie between my breasts. I am swallowing
pills in a dark room, listening to Patsy Cline on cassette. It is not a joke
I expect you to laugh at because romanticizing Xanax isn't funny
and cowboys sort of suck. But I don't want to look the truth in its ugly
doe eyes. I'd rather pretend I am going to feel this good forever,
swaying like a saloon door in the Wild West of my living room.

U

I will kiss anybody who tells me they like my cowboy boots.

In *The Collected Works of Billy the Kid*, Michael Ondaatje writes
"In Boot Hill there are only two graves that belong to women
and they are the only known suicides in that graveyard."

I am not afraid to die. I want you to be happy for me.
I pace the aisles at Shoppers Drug Mart but there is no card for this occasion.

How like the poet. To rewrite its own tragedy into a comedy.

What is a joke but trauma bleeding from the back, stabbed with an exclamation mark?

At a party, I ask a stranger if he will come outside with me
for a cigarette. *I don't smoke but I'll keep you company* he says. I sigh.
It's not me that needs the company, it's the misery.

When I was ten years old I took three Kokanees and drank them in the back yard.

I did not like the taste but I persevered with my prepubescent lagers in the moonlight.

Cowboys are to liquor as Judith Butler is to gender. I'm talking household names.

Why a cowboy? the stranger asks. Because their drunkenness is close to godliness.
What girl doesn't want to be admired for the halo of the toilet bowl around her head?

Cowboys don't need to learn to love themselves. *To come home to themselves.*
Cowboys spit on self-help books and curse 'em like the day they were born.

The badassery of masculinity is well-established in the literary Wild West.
Forgive me, but I am too tired to subvert a genre. I am not the cowgirl for the job.

Why a cowboy? he asks again. I am sick of repeating myself.
I'm a fucking cowboy because I said so. There is no Gender Trouble here.

I am not afraid to die but I do not want to be a suicide in Ondaatje's graveyard.

We believe cowboys. They don't need to explain themselves
over and over again. A cowboy goes to the doctor with a bullet hole,
not a list of symptoms with no exit wound!

∪

I feel like there is something wrong with my skeleton.
I feel like someone has removed my batteries. I called a helpline
but the Duracell Bunny has yet to arrive and assist me.
I feel like I am going to receive a cease-and-desist from the Duracell Bunny.
I feel like soon I will cease to exist; I measure myself smaller once a month.
I feel like I am covered in rust. I'm in my twenties and not a tin man!!
                    Doctor, this can't be right?
I feel like the "meaning of my life" must have gotten lost in the mail.
                    Perhaps there was a party I didn't RSVP to?
I feel like the life of the party has suicidal tendencies.
I feel like my friends are text messages I can't find the words to respond to.
I feel like there is something wrong with my eyes; I can hear myself blinking.
I feel compelled to close my eyes and count to ten while I am driving
or the devil will take my soul. Doctor, do you think you could run blood work
to check my soul count? The devil may have taken it when I was seven
and I failed to do twelve consecutive bunny hops on my scooter.
I feel like the outcome of an early space mission, drifting along
the edge of the atmosphere long after the astronaut dog inside has died.
I feel like I am sleeping even though I am awake, sitting at my desk
staring at my computer like an idiot because who the fuck goes on WebMD?
                    I feel like my fire has gone out. Actually screw that.
                    The crotchless panties of that metaphor are too easy,
                    I'm worried you will think everything is my fault
because I dressed for the part. I mean, who the fuck writes poetry?
I feel like I should be more specific—Sputnik 2 and the dog's name was Laika.
Once, Laika was told she was a good girl and she really believed it.
She shook hands with powerful men for treats and wagged her tail
before embarking on the first doggy-style space mission.

4

Doctor, do you think the problem is me or my environment?
Doctor, do you think I should feel worse for the dog or the spacecraft?
I feel like you are going to give a name to these symptoms
and I will learn to live with it, dress myself with my back
turned toward it in the corner of the room.

U

Stay Home Club is a clothing brand that promotes a culture of loneliness. My favourite shirt features an illustration of a fluffy cat with its paws wrapped around a cartoon heart with the words *I Will Destroy Everything You Love*. And the fun doesn't stop there. You can shop products with sayings like *Crushed by My Own Hopes and Dreams* and *If You're Wasting Your Life Say Hi*. I love their apparel. Half-nihilist, half-existentialist, a teaspoon of melancholia and a squirt of sriracha.

Stay Home Club is a brand that says: I am choosing to be the way I am (however wrecked that may be) and I am wearing it proudly. I am turning the worst parts of myself into a cute slogan on a cotton blend. My first Stay Home Club purchase came with a wallet-sized card that reads *Stay Home Club - Lifetime Member*. I didn't realize that by buying a shirt I was in fact joining the club, let alone becoming a member for the rest of my life.

Membership is to Club like Diagnosis is to Mind/Body.

I will destroy everything you love and then I will destroy myself.

U

Google attention-seeking behaviour in women.

Seek respect, not attention. It lasts longer.
You're an attention whore on Facebook. Please enlighten me about your clinical depression.
Attention-seeking behaviour is the leading cause of being ignored.
Let's have a moment of silence for all those people dying for attention.

Google attention-seeking behaviour in cats.

If the behaviour is due to an underlying medical issue, the cat
may be seeking your attention as a source of comfort from her pain.
It can also be because she's confused by her discomfort.

U

O discomfort, all tooth and claw. Perhaps I too am confused by it. There is something sick and wrong with a woman who seeks attention i.e. I am a grease trap that requires hourly cleaning i.e. I am a misfire shooting for the moon and landing teary-eyed in your living room i.e. I am a vacancy sign flashing its neon tits i.e. I AM I AM I AM.

∪

I have other words too. Other words
other people have given me. Etc., etc.

Each one shivering like a room without a thermostat.
Each one like I am too stupid to put on a coat.

I just want to eat my peanuts and talk
about the weather like everyone else.

i.e. If you are depressed, then why are you at this bar drinking beer with me?
i.e. I get sad too sometimes. It doesn't mean I use it as an cxcuse.

∪

There is an hour-long wait at the fancy breakfast place. I'm starving
for hummus and eggs and to sit across from you and an Americano

and to talk about the rest of the afternoon, so lazy we could fill it with fucking.

We go to the bookstore and in the Western section I flip through paperbacks
once held by men with complexes I am trying to understand.

Amidst stacks of stray self-help I find a book *A Dictionary of Symptoms*
published in 1968. My excitement isn't contagious but you catch it anyways
because I throw it at you as we walk down the street.

A mid-century version of WebMD. I don't think the internet has poisoned us,
rather we have loved arsenic for a long time. Late at night I browse Etsy

for *Poison Rings,* jewelry meant for outlaws to hide their killer concoctions
in. I collect things from the past because I can't hold the future

in my backpack. I tell you the Westerns are for research—
XANAX COWBOY sits on my tongue like loose tobacco.

I flick it at anyone who asks what I am working on.
I'm troubling the romanticization of addiction and the Wild West,
while exploring attention-seeking behaviour and SEO.

In *Bluets,* Maggie Nelson writes "I have enjoyed telling people
that I am writing a book about blue without actually doing it."

Likewise, I have enjoyed telling people I am writing a book
called *XANAX COWBOY* while I slip into the leather chaps

of character. Scattered across my office, the Westerns continue to collect dust.
The eggs are delicious. I love a dish that is impossible to fuck up.

∪

Do you think I want attention? I do. I do.

Why else would I be here salting my wounds like an egg.

A broken yolk and yes before I really cracked.

◡

Cento with lines from Westerns, Sylvia Plath's *Ariel*, lyrics from Patsy Cline songs
& the WebMD page on Xanax

Get ready, little lady. Hell is coming to breakfast.
Though it helps many people, this medication may sometimes cause addiction.
I am nobody; I have nothing to do with explosions.
I love you so much, it hurts me. And there's nothing I can do.
I've got the records that we used to share and they still sound the same as when you were here.
I am nude as a chicken neck, does nobody love me?
Xanax is one of the most commonly prescribed and misused benzodiazepines.
But it shimmers, it does not stop, and I think it wants me.
You look like somebody just walked over your grave.
Dying is an art, like everything else. I do it exceptionally well. I do it so it feels like hell.
The moon sees nothing of this. She is bald and wild.
It ain't dying I'm talking about, it's living.

U

A Xanax Cowboy does not yield relevant results on Google.
By this, I mean there is no *promo code: cowboy.* There is no sex tape scandal.
She's a Xanax Cowboy and not a reverse cowgirl and don't you
forget it. There is an SEO joke. *That you hide a dead body on the second page of Google.*
Where then, am I to keep my living body? How then, am I to live?

⌣

Billy the Kid is more than a Wild West personality, he is a legend
that never dies. Think of him as a ghost—chains rattling the cultural needs of an era.

"Discovering the Kid throughout the years since his death in 1881 has usually meant
discovering the appeals of the West and the Western, the historical landscape and the aesthetic
context within which the Kid both resides and rides. Such appeals continue to preoccupy us
and beckon to us, even though we no longer confront the conditions of the frontier existence."

I'm looking for a frontier on my iPhone's GPS
but only find familiar franchised grease, gas stations
and convenience stores. Red Bull—I only wanted
your wings—was that too much to ask?

There are hundreds of books and movies about Billy the Kid's life and death.

I tend to the online versions of myself
while my body decays.

It's impossible to separate the actual person from these narratives;
it's impossible to distinguish between the events of his life and his legend.

Long outliving the outlaw.
Long live the outlaw.

The legend of the Kid "reveals more than just a century's worth
of infantile egos escaping into the thrilling and uncomplicated days
of yesteryear to avoid the complexities of the present."

I have traded my Doc Martens for cowboy boots.

I am embarrassed by how obvious I am—
like Western dimestore novels that transported men to a simpler time
when they could imagine themselves heroes and forget their wives and briefcases.
O, to turn a page and teleport to the frontier of the American Dream.

In the Wild West there are no emails to answer.
I do not feel the price of gas throb like a hangnail.
There are no pills that promise to cure the world we live in.

"The legend [of Billy the Kid] has varied considerably in accordance
with the changing concerns, values, and aspirations of a particular period."

Billy the Kid, maybe you are not so different from a diagnosis then.

∪

Patient Health Questionnaire (PHQ-9)
Over the last two weeks, how often have you been bothered by any of the following problems?
(answers collected from Michael Ondaatje's *The Collected Works of Billy the Kid*)

1.   *Little interest or pleasure in doing things*

     Blood a necklace on me all my life

2.   *Feeling down, depressed, or hopeless*

     She / had collected several wild and broken animals that, in a way,
     had become exotic by their breaking

3.   *Trouble falling or staying asleep, or sleeping too much*

     Last night was dreamed into a bartender
     with an axe I drove into glasses of gin lifted up to be tasted

4.   *Feeling tired or having little energy*

     The wind picked up, I was drowned, locked inside my
     skin sensitive as an hour old animal

     the sun turned into a pair of hands and began
     to pull out the hairs in my head

5.   *Poor appetite or overeating*

he would have cut off his left hand with a knife to have
something to eat, but he realized he had lost too much blood / already

6.   *Feeling bad about yourself—or that you are a failure or have let yourself or your family down*

Think of the dark air going up through the nose, down to the
stomach rolling around on itself, and then up and out like a
fountain spilling through his teeth hissssssssssssssssssssssssssss

7.   *Trouble concentrating on things such as reading the newspaper or watching television*

get away from me yer stupid chicken

8.   *Moving or speaking so slowly that other people could have noticed? Or the opposite—being so fidgety or restless that you have been moving around a lot more than usual*

I am very still
I take in all the angles of the room

that is why I can watch the stomach of clocks
shift their wheels and pins into each other
and emerge living, for hours

9.   *Thoughts that you would be better off dead or of hurting yourself in some way*

In Boot Hill there are only two graves that belong to women
and they are the only known suicides in that graveyard

If you checked off any problems, how difficult have these problems made it for you to do your work, take care of things at home, or get along with other people?

With his rifle in his
hands he watches the darkness, trying to make out the shape
that is moving toward him

∪

ANXIETY & DEPRESSION contradict each other. Which is to say I have little interest in life—its oil changes and paperwork—yet I can't leave my apartment without unplugging the appliances or go to bed without checking the doors are locked at least three times and then checking to see if I inadvertently unlocked the doors while checking to see if they were locked. Which is to say you shouldn't believe me. Who would fall for a narrative with this many holes? Even if it is my favourite sweater, I should throw it out already. Which is to say we don't like women who contradict themselves, who can't pick a story and stick with it. Why believe a story that can't be proven with bloodwork? Which is to say I'M AN IDIOT WHO TANGLED HERSELF IN BARBED WIRE AND IS TOO LAZY TO LOOK FOR WIRE CUTTERS.

U

XANAX COWBOY: The Motion Picture, Scenes 1–4

3.2   She approaches the bar and a jar of pickled eggs.

1.4   An acoustic version of "Free Bird" sung by Willie Nelson.

1.0   She does not want to ride her horse today.

                Instead she lies in a field amid dung and flies.

2.3   A sunset in the distance. Acrylic on plywood. The orange will fade with the credits.

1.1   She keeps shooing the crows away. Yells *stupid birds I'm not dead yet.*

                It is a comedy at times.

2.1   This is accomplished with careful camera angles.

4.0   In a small room above the saloon. She kicks off her boots and climbs into bed.

3.1   The Xanax Cowboy can weep in her trailer after filming. All hot curler and mascara.

4.1   Mirror above the dresser is covered i.e. she doesn't want to look at herself these days.

3.3   She takes a bite and her mouth fills with blood.

3.0   It is a sad day in the saloon. No drunk men to call her *darling.*

4.2   Pan of milk on the windowsill for stray cats.

1.2   What would you say if I told you animals were harmed during the making of this film?

2.0   The Xanax Cowboy stumbles through the town which appears to be filled with people.

3.4   Forgetting that the pickled eggs are props.

2.2   She tips her hat and waves at cardboard cutouts.

1.3   The soundtrack loosely based on a dream the director had about Quentin Tarantino.

4.3   The Xanax Cowboy is sleeping alone. She performs her own stunts.

3.5   Remembering the eggs are props, she spits and smiles for the camera.

U

PILLS PILLS PILLS has flashed on the marquee of modern medicine for decades. Pills are what replaced psychosurgery. Lobotomy may feel like a cruel and archaic practice, one we can relegate into the dark history of psychiatry. But in 1949, Egas Moniz won the Nobel Prize in Medicine for it. Not only was it the current best practice, it was a winning one. My pills do not have such an impressive CV.

In my early twenties, I spent many nights Googling lobotomies. I didn't think I could live with my brain anymore and I romanticized someone disconnecting my frontal lobe from the rest of me. *Where to get a lobotomy in 2012.* It is not my intention to take this lightly. It is simply my search history.

U

PILLS: Brought To You By *PHARMACEUTICAL FLAKES* ©

Part of a chemically imbalanced breakfast!

U

I want to create a series of paintings inspired by old anatomy posters. You know the kind I'm talking about, where the insides of a woman are visible as if someone has taken a scalpel and cut away the top of her flesh. In these posters, the woman's head is always turned sideways at such an angle you would assume her neck is broken, yet she is smiling. Perhaps the woman does not know that her neck is arranged at an impossible angle; perhaps she does not know what the scalpel has done; perhaps she is afraid to stop smiling because the doctor will ask her why she isn't.

I want to draw anatomy posters like this but with arrows that point to the upsets of my organs caused by different medications, some of which I have been told are impossible. In my anatomy poster for Celexa, there are arrows pointing to my intestines and asshole. I sit smiling in the cold chair at the doctor's office, explaining how blue liquid shot out of my ass ten minutes after I drank a bottle of Gatorade. *That is impossible,* he says. I ask him if he would like a demonstration but he says he does not have time. The side effects are said to go away after a few weeks, but never do. In this poster there is a bright blue river flowing through my intestines. My neck at an angle as *impossible* as the rapids of Blue Gatorade rushing through me.

In my anatomy poster for Zoloft at 50 mg, there are also arrows pointing to my intestines and asshole. I no longer drink Blue Gatorade and I've shit my pants enough times in public that I've learned to take Imodium before I leave my apartment. Like a bear plugging its ass to hibernate for winter, I prepare my ass for the cruel season of the SSRI—its frequent and unexpected shitstorms. Is this a kind of evolution?

On Zoloft at 200 mg, there is an additional arrow pointing to my brain. I call my doctor to tell him I've developed psychic abilities and can see the future in my dreams. He tells me this is not a side effect before hanging up the phone. I continue to see the future and it terrifies me. I keep a journal and while I sleep the future presents itself to me like a woman opening her robe to reveal her bush and breasts. The doctor asks *do you actually see a nude woman, her bush and breasts?* I explain that no, it is a metaphor for how the future reveals itself to me in my dreams. He says he doesn't understand metaphors and continues to talk about the chemical imbalance in my brain. Broken. Neck. Smiling.

My poster for Effexor points towards my tongue and eyes. I swallow half of the minimum dose and two hours later my pupils dilate to the point that I am unable to focus and my boyfriend finds me curled between my desk and the radiator, shaking and sweating. When I speak I sound like I am stuck on fast forward—I can't seem to return my mouth to a normal setting. I am taking Intro to Acting and can't miss my exam. My boyfriend takes me to the university, where I recite a monologue in which I portray a woman who is losing control of her mind. I get an A+ and am told my performance is convincing, with my wild eyes and shaking voice. I return home and do not sleep for 36 hours. I feel like a ghost—out of focus and unable to focus. I'm not sure what I am haunting or why.

With my poster for Concerta, I don't want to draw a woman cut open and smiling; I want to draw a skeleton instead. I have no appetite. I can feel my body starving and I stand at the kitchen counter, shovelling spoonfuls of peanut butter into it. I become so thin my body scares me—I could be a Halloween decoration, dangling throughout October on my neighbour's lawn. A friend is quick to remind me there are women who would kill themselves to be this thin. I feel guilty. To look so close to dying.

⋃

Alcohol eclipses the liver; serotonin eclipses my lack of it.
Once, I drank too much and nearly eclipsed myself. I'VE BEEN SWALLOWED
BY PILLS is an eclipse I spit at the bathroom mirror as shadows chew my face.
I can see the future like rotten fruit. Thou shan't fuck with me.
My nightself eclipses my morningself with two half moons beneath my eyes.
Thou see my flared nostrils? I am a bull raging against herself.
My mind is a china shop and I'm paying for what I've broken. Ha.

I have a theory I must already be dead because what is a life without crying
or cumming? I'm dry as Chicken Delight. Thou shan't fuck me.
An eclipse is a wound like blood on my cactus crotch.

An eclipse is the future covered with fruit flies i.e., my morningself is a rotten pear.
I'm ripe for the wastebasket with tissues and crumpled tears. You know
in another life I was a prophet—men licked my toenails, hallucinated
and begged for the clippings. And NOW? Now I pay a person with a Bic pen
to listen to me speak. Ha. I'm paying for what I've broken.

U

I already told you Zoloft makes me shit my pants. What I didn't tell you is that I joke with friends about how lucky I am to work from home and answer emails on the toilet because humour is the dagger I wipe my ass with. The DOCTOR does not believe me—I must be exaggerating.

I think of performance art similar to the episode of *Sex and the City* where Carrie meets famous Russian painter Aleksandr Petrovsky at a gallery and she is unimpressed by the artist who sits on a ledge above a ladder of knives and refuses to eat. Carrie tells Aleksandr she thinks the woman must climb down from her serrated rungs at 3 am and go to the diner across the street. And so Carrie and Aleksandr visit the gallery in the middle of the night and when they arrive they find the starved artist with no blood on her heels or cheeseburger on her breath.

I imagine myself creating an exhibit called CRAP FACTORY in which I spend 24 hours on a toilet in a gallery without flushing. And at 3 am the DOCTOR will enter to confirm my commitment to wellness and he will gag on the stench and I will shrug and wipe RX#9478638 on the wall in shit. I don't believe critics will respond positively to my crap factory—imagine the headlines: NOT STARVING BUT SHITTING FOR ATTENTION.

I have a tattoo below my hip bone that reads *Welcome to the Machine*. I don't need to explain myself to you, but at eighteen I loved Pink Floyd and decided *Wish You Were Here* was too slutty. Once, I had a man tell me my tattoo was *anti-feminist* and I was commodifying myself as an object. To which I replied *throw a quarter in and fuck me up daddy*. I am sick of having my body explained to me—I am the one living with this machine. So FUCK YOU DOCTOR, FUCK YOU MANCHILD who I drank a bottle of wine with beside a duck pond. These aren't your cogs, and despite what you say I am still churning.

∪

Have I built a house I do not want to live inside of?

Maybe the screws are loose because I have drilled and drilled

too many times, looking for something inside myself that is not there.

∪

Like any girl in her mid-twenties, I think Montreal might save me.
Like a Heather O'Neill character I'd learn to speak in similes so devastating

the pigeons on the windowsill would weep. I move into an apartment
with high baseboards and stained-glass windows. In the winter
the living room is cold and I find holes in the stained glass

stuffed with paper towel to keep the snow out. A Heather O'Neill character
would make wet angels on the hardwood floor. She would shiver

in her tattered nightgown and grind her ass against the cold shoulder
of our cruellest season. A Heather O'Neill character would embrace
the cold like a flea-covered cat and dress it in a velvet bow tie.

I'm getting my MA in English at Concordia. Sometimes I go to class
but mostly I don't. When I do, I bring whiskey in a Thermos, give seminars
on books I didn't bother to read. A professor calls me into their office

and confronts me—*you seem like you don't want to be here.* I tell them
about my broken windows and after that they treat me like an injured bird.

Men wink at me in a language I don't understand
and I smile; it's embarrassing how lonely I am—entertaining men
with nicotine mouths because I cannot entertain myself.

A Heather O'Neill character would never say such a thing
because solitude is the best friend she smokes cigarettes on the fire escape
with; solitude is the nude photo of herself she masturbates to.

On the roof of the apartment across the street there is an injured pigeon
and I think about scooping it up in my palms, building a shoebox nest

and repairing its wing with a splint made from a tampon applicator.
I think about becoming a Heather O'Neill character, skipping down the street
and returning my library books in a hardshell suitcase. Wearing a tutu

to the bar and leaning against the jukebox where men with crooked teeth
line up with quarters hungry for the chance to dance with me.

I think about how I will respond to emails from friends
asking how I am doing in Montreal—*I am so well you could drown in me.*
My life is so sweet here it would rot your teeth.

∪

An Email Exchange between a Thesis Advisor and a Xanax Cowboy

RE: Where Is Your Thesis?
RE: Pigeons Have Tear Ducts but Not Sadness.
RE: Have You Written Your Thesis?
RE: I Feel Like a Sad Pigeon.
RE: You Are a Graduate Student Not a Pigeon.
RE: I Am a Xanax Cowboy What Do You Expect from Me.
RE: I Thought You Said You Were a Pigeon.
RE: I Thought You Said I Was Not.

RE: Have You Started Your Thesis?
RE: If Not from Sadness Then Why Are the Pigeons Crying?
RE: I Will No Longer Indulge Your Pigeon Talk.
RE: I Want to Write a Metaphor with a Lasso.
RE: I Don't Believe You Have Started Your Thesis.
RE: I Don't Think I Can Say a Lasso Is a Noose.
RE: Why Can't You Say a Lasso Is a Noose?
RE: What Happened to the Horses.

U

XANAX COWBOY: The Motion Picture, Scene 5

The Xanax Cowboy has fallen in love. She doesn't care that he is a cruel man who shoots wild horses because he will not tolerate anything he can't tame. He lives in a large farmhouse surrounded by acres of land. The Xanax Cowboy is tired of her room above the saloon. Her life smells like cigarettes and whiskey. She wants to live in the farmhouse, where her life will smell like thunderstorms and fresh bread. When he asks her to move in she packs her suitcases and sits outside the saloon waiting for him to take her to her new life. A papier-mâché moon hung by wire is slowly dragged across the set to illustrate a long passage of time. The pulley is rusted and the moon jerks like a dying animal. Eventually, the Xanax Cowboy takes her suitcases back up the stairs to her life above the saloon. Perhaps he could smell it. How desperate she was to be tamed. The Xanax Cowboy decides to go to lie in the field with the wild horses he has killed. When the scene is over the Xanax Cowboy refuses to go back to her trailer. She stays and strokes the rotting bodies and when the cameras are gone she allows herself to cry.

U

One lasso is hung on a hook by the door.

One lasso is around the neck of a horse, reeling it in like a stubborn fish.

One lasso is a student loan. Another is the bills you can't afford to pay.

One lasso was used in a Lana Del Rey music video.

One lasso is a teenage girl sitting on the curb in suburbia with a Big Gulp.

> She shivers in her hoodie and waits patiently for her life to begin.

> She twirls her hair and imagines being photographed in sepia.

One lasso is a pack of stray dogs. They make a circle with their teeth.

One lasso is a halo of rope and dear god what a drunk and feisty angel.

One lasso is the zip tie around your wrists and now there is nerve damage.

One lasso strangles. A mangled horse limps through the field.

One lasso is a Hollywood reimagining. A Warner Brothers prop collects dust

> in a storage locker outside Los Angeles.

One lasso is the teenage girl who thought her life would be a music video.

One lasso is a bruise in the bathroom mirror and you stroke it like a cat.

Another is a mother who worries too much.

One lasso wins all the blue ribbons at the county fair.

One lasso loses slack in the field while the horse lies down.

One lasso is a long bus ride home with your head leaned against the window

       thinking about the soundtrack.

One lasso asks was that ok and of course it was. *Of course it was.*

One lasso is coiled in the corner of the stable like a snake.

Another is the mother you tell not to worry so much.

Another is a soundtrack that loops and loops.

∪

XC is dizzy like cartoon birds. [Looping / a Lasso]
XC goes to bed with a lit cigarette. [Repetitive]
XC goes to bed with a glass of whiskey. [Repetitive]
XC wakes up and does not remember falling asleep. [Repetitive]
[Rephrase] XC does not make a conscious decision to fall asleep.
[Rephrase] XC loses consciousness like a set of house keys.
XC wakes up after losing consciousness. [Repetitive]
XC wakes up with a burn hole in the mattress. [Repetitive]
[Rephrase] XC wakes up on a mattress with many burn holes.
XC wakes up with bedsheets soaked in whiskey. [Repetitive]
[Rephrase] XC wakes up with a personality soaked in whiskey.
XC doesn't care if you are bored of this shit.
XC repeats these steps. [Looping / a Lasso]

[Looping / a Lasso] *Choke me a little bit* one might say, trying to impress the lasso. This is very stupid. Do not try and impress a lasso. Like a great ring of fire the lasso burns burns burns around a throat leaving rope burns burns burns.

[Repetitive] Like a great ring of fire the lasso burns burns burns around a throat leaving rope burns burns burns like a great ring of fire the lasso burns burns burns like a cigarette that falls from fingers it burns burns burns what it touches with burn burn burn holes like a cigarette that falls from fingers it burns burns burns holes like a lasso it burns burns burns around a throat leaving rope burns burns burns like a great ring of smoke a great ring of smoke a great ring of smoke the lasso burns burns burns.

[Rephrase] The lasso is getting tighter. Don't you see it is going to break your neck? A lasso does not choke a little bit. A lasso chokes you until you aren't recognizable anymore.

U

WIKIHOWDY PARTNER | WIKIHOW ABOUT THAT

WIKIHOW COME THEY SAY THE WEST WAS WON WHEN ALL I SEE IS LOSS

WIKIHOW COME I CAN'T STOP PRETENDING I LIVE IN A WESTERN

WIKIHOW DO I TIE A LASSO IT KEEPS COMING OUT LIKE A NOOSE

WIKIHOW TO BE WELL | WIKIWHAT IS A WELL BUT A SITE TO DROWN IN

WIKIHOW COME YOU AREN'T ANSWERING MY QUESTIONS

WIKIWHY DO I TRUST YOU | WIKIWHY DON'T I TRUST MYSELF

WIKIWHY CAN'T I SHUT MYSELF OFF I WISH I WERE A TELEVISION

WIKISEE COWBOYS IN THE TELEVISION | WIKIWHY CAN'T I BE MORE LIKE THEM

WIKIKEEP TRYING TO RIDE INTO THE SUNSET BUT THE BEAUTY OF IT ESCAPES ME

WIKIHOW DO I GET RID OF THE TUMBLEWEEDS IN MY BRAIN

WIKIWHY ARE THERE COYOTES HOWLING INSIDE ME

WIKIWHY AM I A GHOST TOWN AT NIGHT I TRY TO SLEEP BUT I AM HAUNTED

WIKIHOW DO I SLEEP AT NIGHT | WIKIHOW DO YOU SLEEP AT NIGHT

WIKIHOWL THAT VOWEL SOUND AND ECHO BACK A BEAST

∪

Sometimes when I can't find a Western to watch, I pretend I am Bart in the *Simpsons* intro—stuck after class, writing my sins on a blackboard. After Homer has driven home with plutonium itching his back and Lisa has made the saxophone her bitch; after Maggie and Marge have barged through traffic with synchronized horns—a song and sequence as recognizable as grief. In the yellow laughter universe there is no trauma. But imagine Bart in therapy, describing the shape of his father's hands. How gently they hold a donut and how tightly a throat.

WIKIHOW IS NOT A THERAPIST WIKIHOW IS NOT A THERAPIST
WIKIHOW IS NOT A THERAPIST WIKIHOW IS NOT A THERAPIST
WIKIHOW IS NOT A THERAPIST WIKIHOW IS NOT A THERAPIST
WIKIHOW IS NOT A THERAPIST WIKIHOW IS NOT A THERAPIST
WIKIHOW IS NOT A THERAPIST WIKIHOW IS NOT A THERAPIST
WIKIHOW IS NOT A THERAPIST WIKIHOW IS NOT A THERAPIST
WIKIHOW IS NOT A THERAPIST WIKIHOW IS NOT A THERAPIST

⊍

Trauma lives in the body like a cowboy lives in the television.
I am trying to tell you that it is always 3 am here and I ache like static.

You may wonder how long I can keep this up. The sad cowboy
aesthetic with a prescription bottle that rattles like a snake. I am relentless
as discomfort. I'll drag myself like a dead horse until you believe it.

∪

My professor says the speaker in my poems is not believable.
There is too much technical control i.e. if she is a pill-popping alcoholic
why can't she let loose—wave sloppy syntax like a lasso above her head?
As if an addict is not caged by what she loves; as if she howls
on the side of the highway like a coyote in heat. I AM I AM I AM
the speaker. These poems feel like the only control I have.

∪

I thought if I was better then I would get better
and I didn't. I should have worked harder. I should have tried harder
when I didn't want to work harder and I didn't take enough pills
or I took too many pills and I'm here so I should have been grateful
and gotten better because things could be worse and I feel worse
for not feeling better, I should have gotten better
and I didn't. I should have worked harder. I should have tried harder.

U

XANAX COWBOY: The Motion Picture, Scene 6

There is trouble in the graveyard on the edge of town. Like the rich are buried with their filth, cowboys are buried with their pistols and someone has been digging up graves to steal them. There is a reward for anyone who catches the graverobber dead-handed. The Xanax Cowboy begins to lie in the graveyard from dusk to dawn. She picks her favourite tombstones and tells them all of her secrets. She masturbates on the mounds of unmarked graves so that the souls who haunt them may know that even though they weren't loved in life they are loved in death. The Xanax Cowboy finds it peaceful here, among the dead. Everything is orderly. The bodies organized and labelled in neat little rows. The graveyard is unlike her room above the saloon, where most days she can't even find the time. The Xanax Cowboy thinks the graveyard would be a nice place to live. She lies nude with silver dollars covering her eyes but she can't seem to pique the interest of the earthworms. A man comes by one night and tells her *you have to be dead to live here*. The Xanax Cowboy smiles and falls asleep as she imagines. When the Xanax Cowboy wakes up, her pistols have been stolen. She smiles again because she knows she is getting closer. The director's assistant is suspended from a tree with a bucket of worms which he drops like rain across her body.

∪

In creative workshop, my writing is criticized as fetishizing suicide. I don't know what to do but apologize—the wolves at the table want something *authentic* and I am very much alive. I'm sorry? I'm sorry. The fangs to the left of me ask if I have read *4.48 Psychosis* by Sarah Kane and I am confused by the implication.

PUNCHLINE: PERHAPS I AM WORTH MORE DEAD.

U

In literature, we are always after the great *authentic*. We want our artists to be wounds we can lick. To be frank, we want some fucking blood. In 2005 James Frey's memoir *A Million Little Pieces* was promoted by Oprah's Book Club and became a *New York Times* best-seller. It follows Frey as he recovers from his drug and alcohol addiction in a private rehab facility. Oprah had described the book as transporting readers *into the manic mind of an addict* i.e. a glimpse at madness from the comfort of the couch. However, much of what Frey wrote was not true, and it didn't take long for internet sleuths to remove flesh from bone. Frey had fictionalized the facts of his addiction and his stay at the facility.

The public felt tricked by Frey. He was not the mad alcoholic they wanted. He was only half the wound he had promised to be. What interests me is that Frey had originally tried to publish the book as fiction but no publisher would touch it. What was unpublishable as a novel became a best-seller as a memoir. We were willing to forgive the lazy writing, the swiss-cheese plot, because it was an account of substance-use disorder at its finest. The great *authentic* dogeared in paperback.

XANAX COWBOY
WANTED DEAD ~~OR ALIVE~~

∪

I've been meaning to phone my mother.
But I want to dance—won't you dance with me
in the Wild West of my living room? Look at my chest,
the bolo tie between my breasts. Look at my waist, small
like a little bitch. There is a reason for this, I swear and/or help me god.
The sun sets early now, there is not enough daylight
to contain me. Look at me dancing, uncontained. In my heart,
uncontained autocorrects to *in containers*. A Western is a container
with cigarette holes in the curtains. I am a container with many moods,
none of which smell like cinnamon. Little bitch, little bitch,
let me in. I swear I can't be reasoned with.

————————

My mother calls but I do not answer.
Instead I drink, drink from my dirty glassware.
Look at me buzzed on the balcony. Look at the cat in the alley falling
in love with a dead bird. I'm a lot of things but not even a little bit drunk;
I'm a liar with hiccups, and what of my chest, heaving?

I'd like to tame her, the cat. Like Sylvia Plath, what do you think of *that*?

And what do you think of these cassettes, this dancing?
Patsy Cline, country divine, I'm afraid to admit this is the only song I know
how to sing; I'm afraid to admit there is a correlation between wild things
and the price of tuna. My heart tries to spell *correlation*
but it comes out *corruption*. I have been so far gone that nothing can save me.
Not even autocorrect and/or a sale on tuna. Hiccup, hiccup.
I'm a little bit drunk and a lot of other things.

The curtains with cigarette holes cannot keep the darkness
from my breasts. Evening, what nice teeth you have, all the better to bite
my nipples with. *Hole* and *soul* rhyme so when I am drunk I can write poems
like a tender little bitch. How else am I to understand vacancy signs?

There is a hole in the soul of the hotel across the street. Look at me
in the light of the vacancy sign with a splatter of neon blood on my face.
A hotel is a container with stained bedsheets; a chair is a container
for unholy souls who can't sleep. Soon, I will forget the only song
I know how to sing. Goodnight, sleep tight. When the moon
comes for me, I swear to god, I'll let it bite. I should really phone
my mother. I can't remember what the reason is.

U

The vacancy of my life in Montreal is like a motel
that is far from the interstate. Am I boring you? Whiskey,
mild salsa, muscle relaxants, and some stupid Western I stream
on 123movies.com. The four horsemen of my apocalypse are depressing,
and who am I to talk. Over the phone, it is easy to convince my mother
I am fine. There is so much weather to talk about. A vacancy cannot be filled
by mild salsa. And I know that. But spice of life is a metaphor
I never understood anyways. I am boring myself.

∪

There is
the self and there
are versions
of the self.

Remember that.

To say
I understand
if you never want
to see me

again
is to apologize
for being
one self

To say
darling
I've changed

with your fingers
crossed behind
your back
is another self
entirely

Sometimes XC is on Instagram
because she wants to be witnessed.

#cowboys-have-the-silver-screen
#this-iphone-will-have-to-do

#LOOK-AT-ME #LOOK-AT-ME #LOOK-AT-ME

#like-caution-tape-around-my-throat
#O-crime-of-wanting-to-be-seen

*

A hashtag
was once a pound sign.
A call for help.

A cry for help
is also a hashtag.

I didn't ask for it and here I am
on a bed of splinters
###########

*

XC on Instagram 1.0

Instagram killed the long-poem star.
[eye roll] [camera] [knife] [shooting star]

#my-attention-spans-wingspan-is-that-of-a-sparrow
#instagram-is-comparable-to-eternity #imagine-scrolling-forever
#perhaps-it-is-the-ultimate-long-poem #perhaps-it-is-a-master-narrative
#like-the-odyssey #imagine-homer-getting-likes-for-each-of-his-quests
#or-corporate-sponsorship #battling-the-cyclops-in-hakim-optical-glasses
#anne-carson-should-look-into-that #or-perhaps-matt-groening
#there-is-an-episode-of-the-simpsons-where-homer-is-homer #duh
#it-is-the-21st-century #everything-is-an-imitation-of-the-real-thing
#why-else-are-poets-applauded-for-authenticity
#why-else-are-we-expected-to-bleed

ALT TEXT: The Xanax Cowboy sits on an old yellow couch beside a potted cactus. She sits facing the camera but her eyes shift sideways, glancing at the cactus. As if she is afraid to take her eyes off it. As if she is afraid of what the cactus might do.

XC on Instagram 2.0

Good girls don't spit they swallow
[pill] [wink face] [tongue] [eggplant]

#the-doctor-prescribed-me-xanax-at-nineteen
#I-thought-I-was-filling-a-prescription-but-I-was-filing-a-life-sentence
#turns-out-being-a-good-girl-feels-euphoric #xanax-took-the-edge-off
#it-softened-me-like-a-sepia-photograph #it-was-salsa-for-the-chip-on-my-shoulder
#but-the-more-I-took-the-milder-the-salsa-got-and-the-more-I-needed
#soon-I-needed-xanax-to-feel-normal #I-was-chipped-and-cracked-without it
#like-some-fucking-humpty-dumpty-I-needed-xanax-to-keep-me-together
#just-so-I could-leave-my-apartment-without-falling-apart
#xanax-is-approved-for-the-short-term-treatment-of-anxiety
#doctor-why-the-fuck-then-did-you-prescribe-it-for-seven-years
#long-term-use-alters-the-GABA-receptors-in-the-brain
#long-term-use-leads-to-addiction #long-term-use-causes-cognitive-impairment
#you-said-my-brain-was-a-bad-apple-the-pills-would-fix-but-they-made-things-worse
#I-used-to-be-bruised-and-now-I'm-rotting-from-the-inside-out

ALT TEXT: The Xanax Cowboy is lying in a bed in a messy room. Fringed jackets litter the floor. She is curled up beneath a blanket with her knees pulled up and her arms around them. The bed frame is made from prescription bottles. It is similar to a DIY Pinterest project with wooden crates.

Who needs friends when you can have whiskey
[hard liquor] [orange heart] [shrug] [skull]

#it's-not-like-I'm-lying-to-you #it's-obvious-this-is-curated
#cowboys-are-supposed-to-feel-alone-so-I-pretend-I-am-a-cowboy
#I-don't-want-to-admit-I-am-lonely-and-alone-implies-a-choice
#like-I-choose-to-spend-my-nights-by-myself-watching-storage-wars
#like-I want-this #getting-off-on-the-smell-of-my-own-vomit
#cowboys-do-not-want-to-be-happy #contracts-prevent-it
#cowboys-are-supposed-to-look-lonely #that-full-moon-kind-with-nothing-howling
#loneliness-implies-a-want #some-burning-thing-I-can't-have
#alone-implies-I-have-set-myself-on-fire #there-is-no-witness-to-this
#but-trust-me-I-am-beautiful-dancing-in-the-flames
#if-to-be-happy-is-to-smile-amongst-the-debris-of-everything-you-are
#then-to-be-a-cowboy-is-to-douse-the-debris-in-liquor
#strike-a-match-and-watching-as-nothing-burns

ALT TEXT: The Xanax Cowboy is sitting on a balcony turned away from the camera. She is a dark silhouette. A full moon looms in front of her. Cowboys are lucky. The moon can be looked at for as long as you would like.

∪

Cowboys with silver scars on their thighs.
Cowboys with no Honky Tonk left in them; cowboys who are all Blues.
Cowboys who can roll a cigarette faster than they can do long division.
Cowboys with an early drinking career.
Cowboys who water their cactuses with whiskey.
Some cowboys ask what is a cowboy?
Some cowboys laugh because only cowboys know.
Cowboys with rows of dead cactuses on the windowsill.
Cowboys who never learned to slow dance.
Cowboys who were never asked to slow dance.
Cowboys who swayed drunk beneath the moon instead.
Cowboys who are a long way from home.
Cowboys who are a long way from a definition of home.
Cowboys who can't define home. It must include some form of roof but what else?
Cowboys who have only a small number of defining moments.
Cowboys who finger themselves at night, bored and wanting to feel something.
Cowboys who know feeling something must feel a bit like feeling alive.

∪

Hey, Google. I stood at the mouth of a yawning
canyon and yelled my name and there was no echo.
What's that about? Sometimes I don't even know why
I'm screaming. Hey, Google. *Google!* Are you listening?
Show me something I can clench between my teeth;
show me the image of a woman windblown in the Wild West
and ask me not to romanticize her landscape—
now again in sepia. Show me an arm's length
and a fistful. Will you explain subjectivity?

Google, I may have been lied to. I didn't ask
for the hashtag but I'm lying on a bed of splinters.
Google, I already said that. Why aren't you listening?
I have questions; I need direction. Hey, Google. *Google!*
Let's get serious. Take me to the nearest whiskey bar.
Take me out of context and leave me there.

⎵

XANAX COWBOY: The Motion Picture, Scene 7

The Xanax Cowboy keeps a collection of cactuses in her room. The producers have placed a small speaker inside each cactus and at night they whisper *touch me touch me touch me*. The Xanax Cowboy has come to understand that the cactuses would like to harm her. The producers have come to find the situation amusing. The Xanax Cowboy has come to believe that the cactuses can live a long time without water but not without blood. The producers have learned to keep a large supply of gauze on hand.

U

I have been told that we live with our choices.
Mine is a terrible roommate. She keeps me up at night.
I can't break character because what if the previous tenants
or landlord installed hidden cameras in the light switches?
What if I am always on camera? I must perform Xanax Cowboy 24/7
like I'm some sort of all-night convenience-store/art-installation
though there is nothing convenient about this, and I don't have potato chips.

The camera is never off because there is the possibility it is always rolling.[1]
I can't watch Netflix or have a bubble bath, make an omelette or call a friend.
I have to live on cigarettes and pills, slow dance with myself
and tip my hat at the moon. It's exhausting, to be in character
all the time. But I would rather do that than admit I have the capacity
to pleasure myself. Admit that I have the ability to change.

---

[1] Schrödinger's Western

∪

I allow myself to socialize occasionally by calling the pharmacy to ask questions.

Why am I stuck between the rock of wanting the drugs that work and a hard place
of thinking pharmaceuticals are bullshit?
Do cats fear they are wasting their lives?
If we consider the formula time × speed, how far will flattery get me?
What if I keep making the same mistakes because it is the only way
I know how to get home?
Why didn't Newton tell us gravity would be this ugly?

∪

I have a theory that cowboys are whiskeysexual.[2]
Yes, they fuck women and leave their hearts broken
or occasionally get rowdy behind the saloon with the other cowboys
in a flurry of unzipped flies. When cowboys have sex
I imagine their flasks are visible on the nightstand
or they hold a bottle of whiskey beneath the pillow and feel it
slosh as they thrust. I imagine cowboys take the walk of shame
to the doctor's office after spending a long night alone
with their one true love. And the doctor sighs and shakes his head
while reaching for lubricant, says *pull down your trousers and let's see
what kind of bottle you got yourself into this time.*

---

[2]   to love being fucked up more than fucking.

U

XANAX COWBOY VS COCAINE COWGIRL

DIRECTOR'S NOTE:

Please think of a Tarantino film.
Slow-moving desert aesthetic. Cacti chic like red
lipstick. Muscle cars, dive bars and a harvest moon
over a highway—vacant as my eyes when I'm three drinks
past the speed limit of unslurred words. In this film, women are vicious
in vinyl booths; they're leaning over jukeboxes in cowboy boots
with jawlines so jagged we forget they don't have autonomy—
we forget they are props, like a crochet tumbleweed
in a storage locker outside Los Angeles.

LIST OF PROPS:

A rhinestone pistol.
A caged and injured bird.
An American flag bikini that was made in Bangladesh.
A tube TV that hacks the phlegm of late-night Westerns.
Two single beds that sound like old bones.
A cowboy hat the colour of a stomach ache.
Oversized sunglasses (large enough to keep a secret).
Electrical cord tied like a high voltage noose.
A woman and another woman.
A record player suitcase.
A bulb at the end.

ACT ONE - No More Depression Naps in the Wild West

A twin-size mattress and XC are the only props on stage.
Women are objects and isn't that fucking delightful? The theatre is dark
like bruised knees and apologies. The sound of tumbleweeds
rolls through the speakers and over the audience's head.

CC   *enters stage left in a cloud of white dust and turns the lights on.*

XC   *wakes up from her depression nap.* What are you doing in my Western?

CC   *hands XC her contract and flops onto the mattress beside her.*

XC   I don't understand. This says you are going to kill me.
         Subtext is hiding behind the curtain dressed like a magician and rightfully embarrassed.
         Mistook allusion for illusion. No time for a costume change until the next act.

CC   Remember when the other kids played cowboys and tried to kill each other?

XC   I would lie in the grass and think of ways to kill myself.
         Subtext pulls a dead rabbit from its hat and throws it onto the stage.

CC   That's right, partner. I'm just here to speed things up.
         This show is going nowhere and the audience wants blood.
         CC motions for XC to follow her as she starts laughing her way to hell.

ACT TWO - Highlights of Lowlifes in a Motel Room

Motel room off-centre of nowhere. CC in a pink Corona cowboy hat and American flag bikini. XC is more of a mood. Two single beds and a tube TV spits static.

CC   What do you think of my pistol?

XC   I think it is very nice. When you pull the trigger, does a BANG banner unfurl?

CC   It seems you are implying that language is dangerous.

XC   It seems that you have never read the comments on my Instagram.

CC   Ha. I'll show you dangerous. You know what happens when I pull the trigger. *agitated and sulking. She paces like a tiger with a toothache.* We should order room service. Might as well go out with a bang.

XC   This is a Motel 8. You'd be lucky to get a Snickers from the vending machine.

CC   You don't always need to be a downer. OH WAIT. *Rolls eyes.* That's the whole point.

XC   *looks down at the warning label tattooed on her breasts.*

CC   *increasingly agitated. Sound of her racing heart fills the stage like a stunned sparrow.* I don't want to kill you. But I think we should at least practice.

XC   Do you like the aesthetic of point blank or distance?

ACT THREE - No Diving or Drowning in Boredom at the Motel Pool

On the stage is a kiddy pool.
The audience is asked to use their imaginations
which can be purchased at concession.

CC suntans nude beside her pool, waxed pussy
purring in the sun. She reads Cosmo *and takes*
a quiz though of course she knows the answer.
She is divine and everyone loves her.

XC has a tumbleweed of a bikini line.
She sits crouched in the kiddy pool,
her arms wrapped around her knees.

CC There's a party tonight on the dark side of town.

XC I don't like parties. I always feel like Subtext over there.
   she motions her head toward the back of the stage, where Subtext is
   stapled into a poorly painted piece of plywood representing a wall cactus.

CC You spend so much time lying around lost in your head
   that you're going to get bed sores. If you loosened up, people might like you.

XC *climbs out of the kiddy pool and her bones creak like a rusty box spring.*
   That's easy for you to say. You walk into a room and everyone imagines Scarface
   burying himself in your tits. They see me and are afraid I'll bore them to death.
   Like I'm some sort of pharmaceutical Medusa with pill bottle curlers in my hair.

CC I wish you would admit that you get off on being your own villain.

XC I guess I always thought I was going to grow up and be somebody,
   not just some body lurching through the night.

ACT FOUR - One Can Die For $9.99

Parking lot in front of tired motel.
CC has brought her portable record player suitcase outside,
and "COCAINE COWGIRL" by MATT MAYS & EL TORPEDO plays
persistently like sand in an eye.

XC   We should stop at Taco Bell on the way to the shootout.

CC   Your last supper will be a Diet Coke and Crunchwrap Supreme.

XC   Depressing, isn't it. I think it suits me. Are you wearing that bikini?

CC   I don't know why you take such offense to my cleavage.

XC   Your breasts don't offend me, CC. But the bruises on them do.

CC   *turns to audience and removes oversized sunglasses, revealing two black eyes.*

XC   Did you enjoy yourself last night? Dancing beside the jukebox
with duct tape over your mouth?

CC   If you cleared some space in your feminist agenda, you might actually have fun.

XC   Ha. I'm fun like a wasp thrashing in a glass of whiskey.

CC   I'd rather be bruised than dead and I like the electricity over my head.
[A FLICKERING BULB FALLS LIKE A NOOSE FROM THE RAFTERS]

XC   Do you know why there is no XC rock ballad? Why I'm a tumbleweed without a tune?
throws the plastic music machine and it shatters like a dream.

CC   Because you're a pill. Now get in the car, the drive-thru closes at eight.

ACT FIVE - Finally a Little Action Am I Right?

The stage is a ghost town like waking up alone at 4 am with a dry mouth.
The buildings are painted with eyes shuttered closed.

The announcer calls Xanax Cowboy and Cocaine Cowgirl on stage.

CC enters to the sound of her anthem and the audience cheers. She is the life of the party,
glamorous in her assless chaps. She reminds the audience of shag carpets
and gangster movie aesthetic and makes them feel alive.

XC wears crust in the corner of her eyes and pleather that squeaks when she walks.
The announcer reads XC's warning label as she stumbles onto the stage
and the crowd boos like a bunch of Halloween decorations.

The audience is suspicious of XC's motives. Rowdy and ready for violence.
they chant IF YOU ARE SAD WHAT ARE YOU FIGHTING FOR?

Those who can afford popcorn throw it and those who can't bite their nails.

XC   Listen to them cheer. They can't wait for you to make a wound of me.

CC   What do you call a group of drunk men screaming?

XC   *turns towards the painted horizon and sees a sea of crows, rows of 'em perched on taut wire.*
         We will call them a murder.[3]

CC   You know, it's not my fault that I am a good time half-full
         and you are a pill bottle half-empty.
         That when the audience hears *cocaine* they think *free spirit*
         like they hear *frontier* and think *freedom.*
         It's not right. But it makes for a good kegger.
         That when the audience hears *Xanax* they think *hysterical women,* a wake
         of them screeching and inventing problems to have something to talk about.
         [PRESCRIPTION BOTTLES ROLL ACROSS STAGE LIKE PLASTIC TUMBLEWEEDS]

XC   You're right, CC. You are wild and I am prescribed. I am a hysterical woman
         trying to hide a history of bored housewives beneath my bolo tie. As if chewing
         tobacco could cover the smell of halved grapefruits and white wine.

CC   I'll miss your wit. *Rolls eyes.* Whatever will I cut lines with now.
         points her pistol at XC like an accusation. She pulls the trigger and a bullet unfurls.
         [STAGE LIGHTS DIM TOWARD THE DARK]

         FIN

---

[3] The director coins the term and creates a Wikipedia page.
The audience may take a moment to question what fictions have been presented as facts.
The audience may squirm in their seats. Sandpaper has been provided for friction.
Feral cats are a colony, vultures are a wake, drunk men screaming are a murder.
It has been typed and so it is true. There is no scroll or tablet, only scrolling on a tablet.
The gods of the internet do not have hands. They found them impossible to keep clean.

∪

When I was living in Montreal
I started writing "XANAX COWBOY VS COCAINE COWGIRL."

Workshopping the poem, I was asked if XC & CC were the same character
(was the play an internal monologue or struggle?).

This was not my intention. I wonder now if perhaps I was reading my future.
Poetry like a palm. The way my life line breaks.

I was writing two versions of myself before I had become addicted to one.

*

When I move home from Montreal it is no longer easy to convince my mother
I am fine. All the exclamation marks that punctuated my texts turn to ash.

I am tattered like a dimestore novel; my nosebleeds at dinner are a red heron.
At night she crawls into bed beside me and says

I wish my dad were still here. He would know what to say.

∪

The Xanax Cowboy walks along the side of the highway.

Dozens of pill bottles drag behind her in the dirt, tied to her ankles with string.

They are like tin cans tied to the bumper of a car after a wedding.

Sitcom laughter won't heal your wounds but it will hide them.

I Googled it, and honesty is important in a healthy relationship.

It's hard to say how bad things were. But the number of times I've lied

is the same as the number of times I've said *trust me*.

∪

TRUST ME TRUST ME TRUST ME TRUST ME TRUST ME TRUST ME
TRUST ME TRUST ME TRUST ME TRUST ME TRUST ME TRUST ME
TRUST ME TRUST ME TRUST ME TRUST ME TRUST ME TRUST ME
TRUST ME TRUST ME TRUST ME TRUST ME TRUST ME TRUST ME
TRUST ME TRUST ME TRUST ME TRUST ME TRUST ME TRUST ME
TRUST ME TRUST ME TRUST ME TRUST ME TRUST ME TRUST ME
TRUST ME TRUST ME TRUST ME TRUST ME TRUST ME TRUST ME
TRUST ME TRUST ME TRUST ME TRUST ME TRUST ME TRUST ME
TRUST ME TRUST ME TRUST ME TRUST ME TRUST ME TRUST ME
TRUST ME TRUST ME TRUST ME TRUST ME TRUST ME TRUST ME
TRUST ME TRUST ME TRUST ME TRUST ME TRUST ME TRUST ME

∪

I'm fine, really; Quentin Tarantino once told me I look beautiful in yellow; two plus two equals jaundice; I don't have a problem; the doctor just got the dose wrong again; I didn't want to go to your stupid party anyways; I lassoed the moon once but I let it go because it was heavy and hurt too much; I only have two drinks a day; things have been going really well; I turned down the part of Leonardo DiCaprio's stunt double in *Once Upon a Time in Hollywood*; because I was busy starring in my own half-ass Western; I've been taking my medication as prescribed; I'm not sure where your Xanax went; I don't know where you hide it; the sky is blue because god was sad when he made it and how else are we to explain rain; if looks could kill I'd have plastic forks for eyes; at night I drive down the highway and shake awake the animals sleeping on its shoulder, wiping the crust of maggots from their eyes with a bleach-soaked rag; I'll call you back; I wish I could come but I can't; you don't need to worry about me; I have everything under control; I'll pay you back; I promise; I promise; I promise that promises are meant to be broken, like wild horses.

U

My life has become so convenient I've lost respect for it.

Do you remember when you had to wake up before 10 am for a McMuffin?
Now, I can have it delivered at 2 pm. Maybe that's what really fucked me up.

SkipTheDishes, it's not your fault I'm an alcoholic but I feel outsmarted and ill.[4]

There are apps and pills for everything. I fear I can no longer differentiate
between my subscription services and my autonomic nervous system;

I fear I have forgotten that my medication is not really a part of me.
If we let something in and it stays long enough, it will change us.

I let in convenience at my fingertips and now look at me.

---

[4] To permanently delete my SkipTheDishes account I must tell their ChatBot why. TV didn't prepare me for
breakups with food delivery apps. I know that if I tell the ChatBot *I met someone else* I will be offered a coupon.
TV didn't prepare me to tell the truth but I type it anyway. *I am trying to quit drinking and this app makes
it easy to have alcohol delivered to my doorstep.* The ChatBot tells me *we will miss you and have a nice day.*
SkipTheDishes, it's not your fault our breakup meant nothing to you, that I can make a new account, introduce
myself as a new woman with the same old habits.

∪

In my next life	I will have bangs.
In my next life	I will use coupons and buy peanut butter when it is on sale.
In my next life	I will take my pills exactly as prescribed.
	I will make no mistakes and the pencils will have no erasers.
	I will not smoke and my lungs will be as clean as my conscience.
In my next life	I will be a children's choir, a Sunday morning, a field of clover.
	I will be an entire fucking forest filled with sparrow-song and scat.
	I will be the bird and the worm and it won't matter how early I rise.
In my next life	I will stay away from knives. I will use my hands as utensils.

Carving a chicken with my fingertips—I will kiss the gizzards and whisper
I love you, even the ugly parts; I will whisper
to myself *I love you, even the ugly parts.*

| In my next life | I will be the daughter that my next-life mother wants— |

I will not call her in the middle of the night because I think I am dying.
I will not drink too much and eat too little at Sunday dinner.
I will be a nurse or a teacher with a gospel of grandchildren for her to hold;
they will say *please* and *thank you* and have little bows in their hair.

| In my next life | I will have more accomplishments than bruises. I will be a shining gold star. |
| In my next life | I will practice the advice I have received in this one—I am keeping |

a notebook; I will bring it with me.

U

I comment on the dead bird by the gate. The next day, on its absence.
That's good, my boyfriend says. The stray cats aren't going hungry.

Every night he says *please come to bed*. Every night I laugh and say *soon*.
It's a joke neither of us finds funny. There is no punchline; a comedian shrugs

and takes a sip of water in front of a silent room. There are only white lines
I inhale until I'm scraping snot from rolled dollar bills and putting it back

in my nose—remembering how I once saw my cat puke and eat it. Still hungry.

I don't know how to explain the vacancy when nothing is left—perhaps
empty like a motel that is far from the interstate or like Norman Bates,
a character who goes on living long after the protagonist has died.

I remember a children's movie, where owls steal the sun and everything is wet
and inexplicably flooding. Maybe it's a bit like that. I am jealous of friends

who only eat dead birds on weekends, who have coping skills like cans of tuna.
I spent my savings account on dead birds and don't have the feathers to prove it.

When I hear my boyfriend rise to get ready for work I pretend to be asleep.
He sighs and pulls a blanket over me before taking his dog to the park,

a plastic bag in his pocket to gather her shit with; the bag will live on forever
in the landfill but I can't keep living like this. Imagine watching the same horror movie
every night—thinking this time, maybe this time, she's going to make it out alive.

I remember what a veterinarian once said, holding my cat on his cold table.
You should be able to feel the ribs but not see them. My ribs stick out like rows of excuses.

It's not me, it's my addiction; I can't come to the phone right now.

That's an excuse when my nose is bleeding and I'm screaming at my mother,
when I miss my nephew's birthday and the special cupcake he made for me.

I can't come to the phone and you're speaking to a colony of stray cats,
flea-bitten and giggling—chanting *dead birds dead birds dead birds.*

∪

The Xanax Cowboy Installs a Meditation App

MA	Visualizations are powerful tools.[5]
XC	I visualize a chainsaw hum-hum-humming a noisy little tune.
MA	In this guided meditation, I ask that you empty your mind
	and follow my voice. I will be guiding you on a journey deep within yourself.
	You may experience resistance or discomfort
	but trust that visualizations are powerful tools.
XC	I am not good at visualizations in meditation.
MA	It is normal for the mind to wander.
	Offer yourself a gentle smile and bring yourself back.
XC	The chainsaw has beautiful teeth; I want to ask about its orthodontist.
	Who is your orthodontist? I ask in my mind's eye.
MA	You are in a forest, sitting beside a river. Admire the strength of its current.
	Look around you and there are hundreds of stones.
	Pick them up and examine them closely.
XC	I collect the stones in my pockets as if I am on the shoreline of my childhood.
MA	Feel the weight of each stone in your mind. What do they represent?
XC	What song was the chainsaw singing?
MA	The stones are aspects of yourself that do not serve you.
	Throw each stone into the river and visualize it sinking
	and being carried away by the current.
XC	But it is too late. I have already filled my pockets with stones.
MA	Allow yourself to let go of the weight you have been carrying.
XC	My pockets filled with stones, I wade into the river.
MA	Breathe deeply, in through the nose and out through the mouth, 1, 2, 3, 4.
XC	I sink slowly and am carried away by the current.
MA	Allow yourself to be inspired by this meditation as you continue with your day.

XC   Humming a noisy little tune, I feel inspired as I draw a bath to scream—

MA   NAMASTE.

XC   under water.

---

[5] for a mind preoccupied with self destruction

∪

This ain't my first rodeo. I know how much is a good time
and how much is passed out on the bathroom floor. And when
it comes to that, my boyfriend will find me with a makeshift bath-mat pillow
cradling my head; he will put two fingers to my throat, brush the hair
from my cheek. To keep me safe from death, my mother used to say
what a silly place to sleep when we drove past broken deer on the shoulder
of the highway. Mother, I am older now and sleeping in sillier places.
And still, I want to believe you. That those deer will stretch and tuck
their guts back in; that those deer will treat themselves tenderly.

⌒

I fell asleep in the bath last week. Mother, these stupid places.
I woke up wrinkled and hungover like a whiskey-drenched prune.
I used to describe my life as borderless but am realizing I don't have boundaries.
I have dead-bird energy. Flying into the glass window of myself. Borderless. Ha.
I need to clean up my act, with Windex, a damp rag and elbow grease.
Mother, these stupid birds. The worms crawl in and out of them.
Borderless like wild horses. Boundaries like barbed wire.
Why are the windows shut? I should open up, live a little.
I'm not sure if this is the window to my soul we are talking about.
Even the kitchen sink has boundaries. Will only hold *so much* filthy water.

Mother, I fear the window to my soul is filthy.
I tried to Google h*ow to clean a window soul*
but it autocorrected to *how to clean a windowsill.*

All it takes is a misspelling of "satin sheets" to be shit on by the devil.

You once told me you drowned in a past life.
Perhaps this is why I am drawn to bodies of water.
When a lake is not nearby a clawfoot tub will do.

∪

First and final seven lines from Sylvia Plath's "The Applicant"

First, are you our sort of a person?
Do you wear
A glass eye, false teeth or a crutch,
A brace or a hook,
Rubber breasts or a rubber crotch,

Stitches to show something's missing? No, no? Then
How can we give you a thing?

———————

I am not your sort of person. My eyes bloodshot, my crotch a cactus.

How am I to show you what is missing when I do not know myself? How? How?

Cowboy is not a pronoun. It's "a man, typically one on horseback, who herds and tends cattle."

I Googled that. I'm not ashamed to admit Wikipedia is a 21st-century god.

I can't select *Cowboy* from even the most inclusive checkboxes that box me in.

I have my own definitions of *Cowboy*. Most of them whiskey-drenched and riding into the sunset.

I tell people I like the pronoun *it* and they laugh. I want to be the weird cousin in the family.

Loneliness takes shelter in the singular.

O childhood of dragging a stick along the fence of recess.

It. A little less human. A little more touch me. An object on the table can't be objectified.

Of course it can. But not for its ass, its tits. *It* escapes the body, a master illusion

floating without form. When I am *it* I put my stick down and am not lonely anymore.

When I hear a mother tell their child *it* is ok in the grocery store,

I pretend they are speaking to me.

I am ok, I think, reassured as I inspect bruised apples.

When I check the forecast and see *it* is expected to rain today, I gather tissues to cry & cry.

I want to be a river but there is no checkbox for that either.

I want to be a thunderstorm, a puddle, the smell of wet grass.

When I was living in Montreal I signed up for a service to borrow bicycles.

A page translated poorly from French to English and I was presented with the checkboxes

of *Man* or *Wife*. I don't know why I needed to be a man or wife to borrow a bicycle.

It took weeks to decide. *Wife* at least rhymes with *knife*. To slice through bread or skin.

To rust when not attended to. I checked the box.

I asked the bicycle-borrowing service, do you take me to be your wife?

It can sew, it can cook,
It can talk, talk, talk.

It works, there is nothing wrong with it.
You have a hole, it's a poultice.
You have an eye, it's an image.
_My_ [bicycle], _it's your last resort._
Will you marry it, marry it, marry it.

U

CC is alone and sad in the static of 4 am.

CC calls XC. Leaves a message *please can I have some pills.*

CC calls everyone she knows (this isn't what loneliness sounds like).

CC can't stand being alone. She lies down and tries to avoid herself.

CC hates when the Wild West goes to rest. She hasn't slept in days.

CC thinks about getting a GIRLS GIRLS GIRLS sign outside her window.

CC is starting to rust. Drugs have a way of taking away your shine like that.

CC calls every number in the phone book (*this* is what loneliness sounds like).

CC lets cowboys from the saloon fuck her if they promise to stay the night.

CC lets cowboys be rough with her if they promise to be tender after.

CC is so lonely she could cry, her heartbeat is so fast she could die.

CC likes getting her little bruises kissed; she thinks this is love.

CC never checks the weather. It's always clouds of shame.

CC has a bloody nose from fighting her demons.

CC feels like a bright thing, spent.

U

Dead birds should not feel as amazing as they do.
At night when I have licked the last wing clean I text the trees
by the river and plead beneath the moon for more. When my mother calls
to ask if I have been remembering to take my medication, I know
what she really wants is to ask about the dead birds. She is listening
for the muffled sound of feathers in my mouth, as if I'm a cartoon cat.
It sounds silly when I say it like that. Dead birds, dead birds, dead birds,
why, why, why am I wasting away, picking clean the carcasses
of dead birds. How many fucking times can I say dead birds.
How many times can I promise to stop eating them only to find
myself scavenging the next day. Knowing they will never love me back
and falling in love with them anyways. I can never have enough
even when I have had enough, can never have too much
even when I have had too much. My heart a hummingbird panicking
in my rib cage and I laugh at the possibility. My heart a dead bird.

∪

My family rented a cabin one summer. It was late August
and I found a nest of goose eggs in the reeds crowding the lake.
I knew the eggs were rotten and no life would crack forth from them.
Still, I scooped them up in my T-shirt and took them back to the cabin
because I was rotten too. I convinced my little brother he could hatch
the eggs and he sat on them for hours in nothing but his swim trunks.

Until my grandfather came outside and said *what the fuck are you doing*.
Until my grandfather hurled the eggs into the lake, where they sank like baseballs.

My brother cried and I watched, giggling, a spectator of my own sport—
thrilled by my brother's tears and the impossibility of his goslings.

———————

Sarah Peters writes that "cruelty is temporary" but I know something of its permanence.

How it perseveres and turns inward as if deep in contemplation.

———————

Cruelty's ragged
brow furrowed, thinking,
                    thinking.

———————

Perseverance, I hear my parents say as I cross the finish line
ahead of my friends, gathered like a flock of geese. As I collapse in the cold grass,
asking for my inhaler. *Our daughter has perseverance.*

————

O to persevere in the cold wind of adversity and asthma.

O the bullshit I must wade through. *Happiness comes from within* swirling around my ankles
like lukewarm letter soup.   Cruelty also comes from within.

————

I am not playing the devil's advocate, no
I am the devil's unpaid intern hosting a webinar

on how to set fire to self-help books in six easy steps.

My shoreline not of sand but sulfur,
stinking like rotten goose eggs in late summer heat.

————

Honk if you hate shit on your windshield?
Honk if you love to shit on windshields?

Why the fuck am I writing a poem about geese and pretending I know the devil.

————

I can't 5K Run for Fun
away from my problems anymore.
I'm not fast enough. I quit.

———

Anne Carson's words are dirt beneath my fingernails: "girls are cruelest toward themselves."

Who else would piss on consequence in the moonlight, their car parked in the ditch.
Or train their body to shake without poison. Like teaching a goose to eat from the devil's hand.

———

There is:

*

cruelty spit
upon others and cruelty
spit upon you.

But what if you could
have your cruelty
and eat it too?

*

Inner cruelty
is the most fun a girl can have

without relying on anyone else.

#crueltyboss

―――――

Hannah, if you're bored then you're boring my grandfather used to say.
I would take my boredom and sulk with it, feed it Ritz Crackers and Cheeze Whiz.

I remember watching a children's movie where a girl finds an abandoned nest
of eggs and she cradles them in her little arms and takes them home to hatch them.

At some point her father runs through a field in his underpants and an evil man
comes and tries to clip the birds' wings. Eventually the girl builds an airplane
that looks like a giant goose so she can teach them to migrate.

―――――

The geese can't change their migration.
They fly where their parents taught them to.

If that ain't a metaphor then show me what is.

―――――

Alright. To clip a bird's wings.
Lack of flight becomes *lost potential.*

My potential is not lost, it is misplaced.

I'm content in my apartment, drinking

my wings into a clipped oblivion,

taking that over some wingspan that could last decades
and then what, tell me, then what.

———————

Boredom may seem harmless but I know something of its teeth.

———————

My boyfriend and I go for ice cream and walk the dog
around the park. At the pond, there is a duckling floating alone.
I try to coax it into my arms but it swims away to follow a family of geese.

At home I curl into my nest of Netflix, thinking about
how that duckling is going to die trying to be something
its not. How it will never be anything but ugly.

———————

Our family albums are saturated with pictures of me at duck ponds
crouching beside the water. My mother says I would wait like that for hours,
my outstretched hands holding bread crumbs. Proof of my *perseverance*.

I don't know when to give up. I don't know what to give up.

Why do childhood photos fuck us up so much.

*

Why does childhood fuck us up so much.

―――――――

Why did that bitch get goslings and I got rotten eggs.

My fantasies were not elaborate. My budget was reasonable.
I wanted to find a wounded animal. Something wild but broken.

A little friend for a girl like me. I never found what I was looking for
because we can't find what we are looking for outside of ourselves, can we?

Turning inward, I became my own wild and broken thing.

―――――――

Do you want to hear something ridiculous?
That movie, the one with the girl who cradles the eggs
in her little arms is based on a true story.

I can't recall a time when I realized my life would not be like a movie
i.e. I still think my life could be like a movie.

My rotten eggs are placeholders.
Something's gotta hatch or happen.
Grandfather, I'm boring.

―――――――

What true story am I based on?
I am afraid to ask, but I want to know how this one ends.

U

XANAX COWBOY Vol. II: The Motion Picture

XC is sad and drinking
alone. Her hat is hung low, shadowing
her eyes. A cowboy is supposed to be drunk
and lonely. This

is not remarkable. But wait (

there's more) .

XC is beginning to feel as if her soul has left her body.
She lies in bed and commands her soul to close the blinds.

STUPID SOUL
doesn't do anything.

XC gets out of bed and shows her soul how to open and close the blinds.

XC spends hours staring at the phone and commanding it to ring.

Aha! Success. CC on the line.

XC has known CC since before they wore drugs as prefixes.

XC knows her soul carried CC down the wires.

CC is worried about XC.

The way she walks around town with the safety taken off of her pistol and life.

Now

XC is
crying.
She does not
make sense. Her words stumble
something about pills

and
sleep
;

something about locking herself in the stable
with carbon monoxide from the horses.

CC asks XC

if she will go to the Crisis Response Centre

(

there is no Crisis

Response Centre in the Wild West

)

.

This scene has been inserted by the reelist.

Her plan to kill herself tonight was to sit in garage to cause carbon monoxide poisoning. Writer attempted to gather further identifying information but Hannah is ++guarded.

We cannot ascertain the reelist's motives

but we can

speculate. Perhaps
bored of the Wild West
it takes footage from XC's life

off set

from a cigar box in its pocket
and uses it to

offset

the film. Reality leaks in like a sad eye leaks out.

(Do not ask how the reelist acquired the footage—

      Do not ask questions
      you do not want answers to

—you will find yourself in a plot hole the size of a grave.)

      is some of the best advice
      available on Pinterest.

Nod your head like there is a wire attached to your frontal lobe running
up through the ceiling and the angels in the attic are afraid of losing their wings.

XC goes and feels like her detached soul, transparent

and stupid.   She is a cowboy
and should not be here; cowboys are supposed to be fucked up a little

bit   raw around the edges.

XC is taken to a white room
and asked questions which she glares at.

Writer completes triage. Writer advises client after triage that writer's sense is that she is intoxicated at current time and that although client is denying any current SI, proper SRA cannot be completed due to level of intoxication. Client tells writer that she wants to go home, that she'll be safe. Writer reiterates to client that writer cannot discharge her...she appears to be actively under the influence.

XC has her pills taken away.
She sits in the waiting room w/o her brain.

She is told she can have her pills and leave
anytime after all she hasn't been admitted yet hasn't admitted

anything
except

that she was hungry
and said egg salad on white [thank you!]

XC is becoming agitated she wants to leave and cannot without her pills
that would be like leaving without an organ.

Writer advises client that 911 will be called if she decides to leave. Client initially in agreement to await in CRC lobby area. However, as evening progresses, client continuously comes to desk requesting her medications and requesting to go home...writer calls WPS and request that WPS come to CRC and consideration be made to take client to IPDA. Writer activates 911.

Hannah refused to have her vitals taken by writer. Hannah presented as irritable, stating "I just need my drugs and then i'm out of here. I've been waiting like an hour and a half to get my drugs."

XC is an outlaw
with her pistols pointed at the Sheriff and the Deputy

[What have ya been drinking tonight]
the sheriff and deputy ask.
[whiskey] XC hisses at the stupidity
of law enforcement.

All cowboys drink whiskey.

*

Two police officers say
[I thought all alcoholics drank vodka].

The reelist has inserted another section of film.

A handcuffed girl is stunned in the back
                                    of a police car
almost as if she was daydreaming
or had momentarily forgotten where/who she really was.

At this point, WPS advise client that she will be coming to IPDA under IPDA act. Client expresses upset re: same, client grabs her purse and tries to leave CRC. WPS at this point physically stop client from leaving and put her in handcuffs and escort her out of the building.

Or
is.   Almost

as if   this is a movie in her mind   as if

she was the reelist the entire time.

Switching between a story she tells herself and reality.
This is her real life, she is the realist.

Do you sometimes tell a story
about yourself and say it happened to someone else?

          Step

back.

          Observe. This is not happening to you.
          This has not happened to you.

*

We tell stories to keep ourselves safe.

Why else this cowboy carapace.
Why else this intoxicated western.

XC's escape
scene has been cut
like a throat by
the reelist

its replacement

is a

wound wound around

the   film.

~~The Xanax Cowboy escapes from jail, walks home rattling with pills the sheriff didn't~~
~~find on her and sloshing back the whiskey she stole from the deputy. The streets are~~
~~empty and the scene is framed in such a way that the sun is rising and the Xanax~~
~~Cowboy is walking toward it and it creates a halo of light around her.~~

Her blood-alcohol level
is found satisfactory at the drunk tank
and they ask her if she would like them to call

her a cab. They ask where she would like to go.

Home, she says.
Do you live alone, they ask?
Yes, she replies.

And they call her a cab.

Because she has her pills in a plastic bag.
Because she is no longer in handcuffs.
Because she is not going to ask for help anymore.

WPS [took] client to IPDA under Intoxicated Persons Detention Act and client will be reassessed by IPDA once sober.

XC calls CC
her sad-sack soul
soaring down the telephone wire
and morphing into a RING RING RING
that CC answers.

CC never sleeps she is
like Seattle or a streetlamp   that burns

day & night & day & night & day & night
day & night & day & night & day & night
day & night & day & night & day & night

with bloodshot eyes.

Now

CC is
crying.

Saying
I know you
won't stop trying to leave
the Wild West and
nobody gets out
alive.

∪

My mother says she could stop worrying,
if only she knew how Xanax Cowboy ends. I know this
is not what she is really asking. How much easier to say
she needs to know how *Xanax Cowboy* ends than to say *when*.
How much easier it is to talk about my book than my life.
But mother, you don't need to worry. When Xanax Cowboy ends
I'll take off my cowboy boots and tell you another story.
The book is over and there is still so much weather to talk about,
there is still so much I have to say, you can trust me.

NOTES

Page 2-3 –
This poem is in conversation with Michael Ondaatje's *The Collected Works of Billy the Kid.*

Page 7 –
The first italicized stanza is composed of phrases taken from Google search results for the query "attention-seeking behaviour in women." The second italicized stanza is taken from Google search results for the query "attention-seeking behaviour in cats."

Page 15 –
"Discovering the Kid throughout the years since his death in 1881..."
"reveals more than just a centuries worth of infantile egos..."
Tatum, Stephen. *Inventing Billy the Kid: Visions of the Outlaw in America, 1881–1981.* Albuquerque, University of New Mexico Press, 1982.

Page 16 –
"the legend of [Billy the Kid] has varied considerably..."
Lenihan, John H. *Journal of American History,* Volume 70, Issue 2, September 1983.

Page 17-19 –
All unitalicized lines are from a questionnaire used to assess depression. All italicized lines are from Michael Ondaatje's *The Collected Works of Billy the Kid.*

Page 24-25 –
This form is inspired by *Tender Points* by Amy Berkowitz

Page 26 –
The refrain of "Ha" is borrowed from "Not Even This" by Ocean Vuong.

Page 34-35 –
This form is inspired by "My Own Private Patriarchy" by Jennifer Chang.

Page 89 –
"A bright thing, spent" is the final line of "Grief, oranges" by Alice Major.

Page 97-110 –
The sections appearing at the bottom of pages are taken from part of my medical record. I obtained a copy in order to contest it, but I was told that I could not rewrite their record of the night. At best, I could have my version of events added to the record. Rather than add my version to their record, I have added their record to my version. O contrast of how that particular evening unfolded. Between what I was told, and what was happening. Between what I wasn't told, and what was happening. Between the stories we tell ourselves, and the stories that are told about us.

ACKNOWLEDGEMENTS

OMG acknowledgements! Here we go. I write *amazing* a lot.

Thank you to my family. You always let me be whatever I wanted to be, and I am so grateful for your love and support.

Thank you to the team at Anansi for making this happen. You are all AMAZING.

Thank you to the crew at CV2, past and present. You are all beautiful nutjobs and it has truly been an honour to be a nutjob alongside you.

Thank you to the creative writing community at the University of Winnipeg. Juice open mics were something special. There is still a glow in my mind when I think about them. Thank you, David Brigole: you have always been such a huge supporter of my work and an amazing friend.

Thank you to the Hunters Writing Collective. I love you all. Special thanks to Molly Cross-Blanchard. Don't puke when you read this because I know it is gross, but you have no idea how amazing it has been for me to see you become the writer you are. Goddamn, are you ever shining. Thank you for working on *Xanax Cowboy* with me. You are an amazing editor. I trust your feedback so much that you are personally responsible for approximately thirty pages being cut from this manuscript.

Thank you, Marika Prokosh, my oldest writing pal. Your work continues to baffle me and maybe one day I'll twist words like you do. Thank you to Eileen Mary Holowka and Chelsea Peters Parkinson for your always thoughtful comments and feedback. I am lucky to know you both.

Thank you, Stephanie Bolster. Concordia is lucky to have you. You care so much for students. Not only for their work, deeply respecting what they are wanting to accomplish, but also their wellness. You taught me vulnerability. I didn't realize that I was writing myself out of my poems, and through you, I learned to leave some of that rawness in. *Xanax Cowboy* owes a great deal of its range to that.

Thank you, Kevin Connolly, for taking a chance on this cowboy. You understood my Wild West from the first time we spoke, and I couldn't have asked for a better editor for this train wreck, because you get that I love a good train wreck. Thank you for all our wonderful phone conversations. Maybe it wasn't so much a train wreck as a train robbery that we executed together.

Thank you, Paul DePasquale and Margaret Sweatman. Paul, you were the first professor to ever read my creative work and you told me to cut the "existential dread." While that comment may seem small, it took a big bite into my approach to poetry. Margaret, you guided me along when I was just starting out as a writer, and I don't know if I would have had it in me to keep going back then without your support.

Thank you, *Room, Prism International, The Malahat Review,* and *Arc Poetry Magazine* for publishing parts of this book or its earlier versions.

Thank you, Irfan Ali, Domenica Martinello, and Jacob McArthur Mooney for selecting excerpts from *Xanax Cowboy* as a finalist for the 2021 RBC Bronwen Wallace Award for Emerging Writers, and for your extremely accurate jury citation, because I reread it when I forgot what the hell I was trying to do.

Thank you Andrew Faulkner and Dallas Hunt for writing blurbs for this book. To both of you—I love your poetry and am honestly just so happy that you have even read my book, and then I can't believe you have said such nice things on top of that.

Thank you! Thank you! (One for each of you).

Thank you to the Manitoba Arts Council and the Canada Council for the Arts for your generous support of this project.

*

My most special thanks to Catherine Hunter and Clarise Foster.

Catherine, you taught me almost everything I know about writing and editing. I remember everything you have taught me over the years, and I put that everything into every poem I write. I found my voice when I was taking one of your classes. I showed you a poem, and you told me that you weren't going to provide feedback on it because you didn't want to derail what I was doing. Things started to click after that. You helped me in my AHA moment, and then continued to help me learn to edit the hell out of my work from there. Thank you.

Clarise, I wouldn't be the writer or the person I am without you. Your encouragement over the years has kept me going. I stopped writing poetry for several years because I didn't think I had anything to say. You encouraged me to keep going. So, I kept going until I realized what it was I had to say. *Xanax Cowboy* would not exist without you. You taught me how to be gentle with myself when I needed it. You taught me to relax and laugh and take a break and come back swinging. Thank you, thank you, thank you <3.

ABOUT THE AUTHOR

I am a Xanax Cowboy what do you expect from me.